AF428255

How Dandy Is Candy?

WRITTEN & ILLUSTRATED
BY
LOREN PSALTIS

HOW
DANDY
IS CANDY?

Who loves candy???
ME!
ME!!!
AND ME!!!

Who loves a treat of sugary goo? You! You!!!
Oh!!! And me TOO!!!

But why oh why do we love sugar so?
Because it tastes good! Don't you think so?!

But do you know what else it does?
All that frosty, syrupy fuzz?

It gives us energy to move and have fun!

But how does it do this? How is it done?

Well it goes from your mouth...
And then it heads south!

But then from your tummy it goes to your brain!
Faster than a car, train or plane!!!

And what does it do when it gets in your head?
Well I'll tell you what the doctors have said...

It sends all its sweetness to your muscles!
To get on with your daily bustles!

Yay! You may say "This sounds just great!"
But "Hey!" I will say, "Perhaps you should wait!"

Because too much sugar is really, really bad!!!
It makes you act silly and a little mad!

But come on for real!!! That's not a good deal!!!

You see the problem is greed,
We eat way more sugar than we really need!

**And did you know it's in EVERYTHING we eat?
It doesn't even have to be sweet!**

**It's in milk and bread, cereal, pizza, pasta and rice!!!
And in vegetables and fruits, which is why they taste so nice!**

And when you get a little too much,
Of all these sugary candies and such,
Your brain gets really confused!
It's too much sugar that can't be used!!!

So you get a little crazy!
Or you feel super lazy!!!

So definitely you should not eat candy every day!!!
You're getting your sugar anyway!!!

But it's nice as a treat once in a while!
But just have one! Not the whole pile!!!

THE END

About the Author

Loren Psaltis was born in 1966 and raised in Johannesburg, South Africa. She moved to the US in 2006.

A voracious reader with an inquisitive mind, Lori was always questioning and learning. Known in her community and beyond for her strength, positivity, kindness and humor, she touched, helped and influenced countless people with her selfless, charitable approach to living. From the young to the old, her infectious charisma and compassion drew in people from all walks of life and backgrounds.

Overcoming a difficult upbringing, personal tragedy and trying circumstances, Lori sought to make the world a better place, bringing her message of love and generosity to all she met. Her professional success in business, extensive travel and extraordinary life experience, coupled with her tireless dedication, helped Lori serve as a bright light to the world, bringing hope and resources to underprivileged children, animal protection and many other worthy causes.

Lori channeled her experiences into writing her first book *The Devolution of Man*, as well as thirteen children's books which she wrote, illustrated and edited herself. Through these books, she hoped and dreamed of spreading a positive message to a wider audience of children and adults.

Loren's tragic and untimely passing in 2021 left a huge void in the countless lives and memories of all those she touched, including her husband and best friend of thirty-six years.

BOOKS BY
LOREN PSALTIS

A MONSTER NAMED BOO

HEY! COME TRAVEL
WITH ME

THE MOUSE,
THE GROUSE, &
THE LOUSE

THE NIGHTINGALE

MY SPECIAL CAT

A CAT NAMED ALLEY

PENGUIN'S JOURNEY

DREAMING IN BED

HOW DANDY IS CANDY

FUN NUMBERS

FOLLOW THE RAINBOW

MONKEY & ROO

JASON'S DREAM